STEP-by-STEP
SCIENCE

Water

Helena Ramsay

Illustrated by Raymond Turvey
and Joanna Williams

W
FRANKLIN WATTS
NEW YORK • LONDON • SYDNEY

© 1998 Franklin Watts

First published in Great Britain by
Franklin Watts
96 Leonard Street
London
EC2A 4RH

Franklin Watts Australia
14 Mars Road
Lane Cove
NSW 2006
Australia

ISBN: 0 7496 2943 6
10 9 8 7 6 5 4 3 2 1
Dewey Decimal Classification 553.7
A CIP catalogue record for this book is available from the British Library

Printed in Dubai

Planning and production by Dicovery Books Limited
Design: Ian Winton
Consultant: Chris Oxlade

Photographs: Bruce Coleman: page 5 (Jeff Foott Productions), 9 (John Shaw), 11 (Hans Reinhard),
24 top (Kim Taylor); Robert Harding Picture Library: page 7, 8, 20, 31; The Hutchison Library: page
12; The Image Bank: page 21, 24; Images: cover; Last Resort Picture Library: 25; Oxford Scientific
Films: 27 (Norbert Wu), 28 top (Mark Hamblin), 28 bottom (Tom Ulrich); Alex Ramsay: page 6, 21;
Tony Stone Worldwide: page 6 (James Nelson), 11 (H Richard Johnston), 13 (Philip and Karen Smith),
15 (Bob Thomas), 19 (Vince Streano), 22 (Hugh Sitton), 30 (Spike Walker). Art: page 30 Stuart Lafford.

Contents

Water, Water Everywhere   4

Liquid, Solid and Gas   6

Making Clouds   8

Water Cycle   10

Clean Water   12

Washing   14

Down the Drain   16

Water Power   18

Floating   20

The Salty Sea   22

Walking on Water   24

Under Pressure   26

Staying Dry   28

Living in Water   30

Glossary   32

Index   32

Water, Water Everywhere

Imagine a world without water! There would
be no plants or animals because every living
thing needs water to survive. Without it
we couldn't keep ourselves or our
homes clean. We couldn't drink,
go swimming or cook.

The Earth is a very
wet place. More than
70 per cent of its surface
is covered by water. Most of the
Earth's water is in salt water oceans.

4

Geysers

Deep under the ground the rocks are very hot. Water seeping through the layers of hot rock turns into high-pressure steam. Eventually, the steam bursts out of the ground as a geyser.

Did you know that there is water inside you, too? Two thirds of your body consists of water. In fact, there is as much water in your body as there is drink in these cans.

Liquid, Solid and Gas

Normally, we think of water as a liquid. But it can also be a gas or a solid. In cold weather water can freeze and turn into ice, which is a solid.

Water can be flavoured with fruit juice and then frozen to make ice lollies like this one. Lollies are good to eat when the weather is hot.

When water boils it turns into an invisible gas called **water vapour**. Look at the spout of a boiling kettle, but don't stand too close or you will be burned! It looks as though there is a space between the spout and the cloud of steam rising from it. This space is full of invisible water vapour.

As the water vapour cools it turns back into tiny drops of water that form a cloud of steam. This process is called **condensation**.

Icicles

When the weather is very cold, water dripping off the edge of a roof can freeze to make icicles. As more water runs off the roof, It freezes too, making the icicles even longer.

Making Clouds

When water is boiled it turns into water vapour very quickly. Water does not have to boil in order to turn into vapour. The cold water in rivers, lakes and oceans turns very slowly into water vapour all the time. This process is called **evaporation**.

When water vapour rises into the air it cools and forms tiny drops of water, which become clouds.

EVAPORATION

1 Find a puddle on a hard surface outside. Draw a chalk line to mark the edge of the water. Come back every hour and draw another line. You will notice that the water in the puddle is slowly drying up.

2 Write down how long it takes for the puddle to dry up. You could do this experiment twice: once on a sunny day and again on a cloudy day. Compare your results.

The Water Cycle

High up in the sky, water vapour from seas, rivers, ponds and lakes cools and condenses into millions of tiny drops of water. In warm climates, these **droplets** join together to make bigger drops which fall as rain.

Vapour cools and turns back into water

Rain falls on the hills and fills the rivers

The rivers flow back to the sea

Water vapour rises into the air

Water evaporates

In cooler places, the water droplets form into crystals of ice and then into snowflakes high up in the sky. As the flakes of snow fall through the air they melt to form raindrops.

A lot of rain-water soaks into the land. This water eventually finds its way back into streams and rivers. Filled with rain-water, lakes, rivers and streams flow into the seas and oceans.

Water evaporates

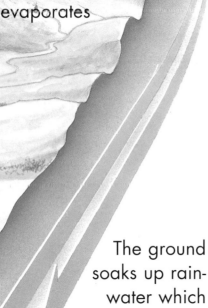

The ground soaks up rain-water which seeps back into rivers and streams

Once the rain has fallen, evaporation begins again. The same water can evaporate and fall as rain again and again. We call this the water cycle.

Acid Rain

Some of the **fuels** that we burn on Earth produce poisonous gases. These gases mix with water droplets in the air and fall as acid rain. Acid rain kills plants and trees and **pollutes** our rivers and lakes, poisoning the creatures that live in them.

Clean Water

All of our water comes from the rain and melted snow that fill rivers and streams. We use water every day in our homes. Large quantities of water are used in factories, too.

Worth Its Weight...

In many parts of the world people do not have running water in their homes. They sometimes walk a long way every day to collect water from a well or a river. Would you use so much water if you had to carry it like this?

Wind pump and bore hole

Water is collected in various different ways. Rivers are **dammed** to make artificial lakes called **reservoirs**. In some places, water is pumped up from a well or a **bore hole**.

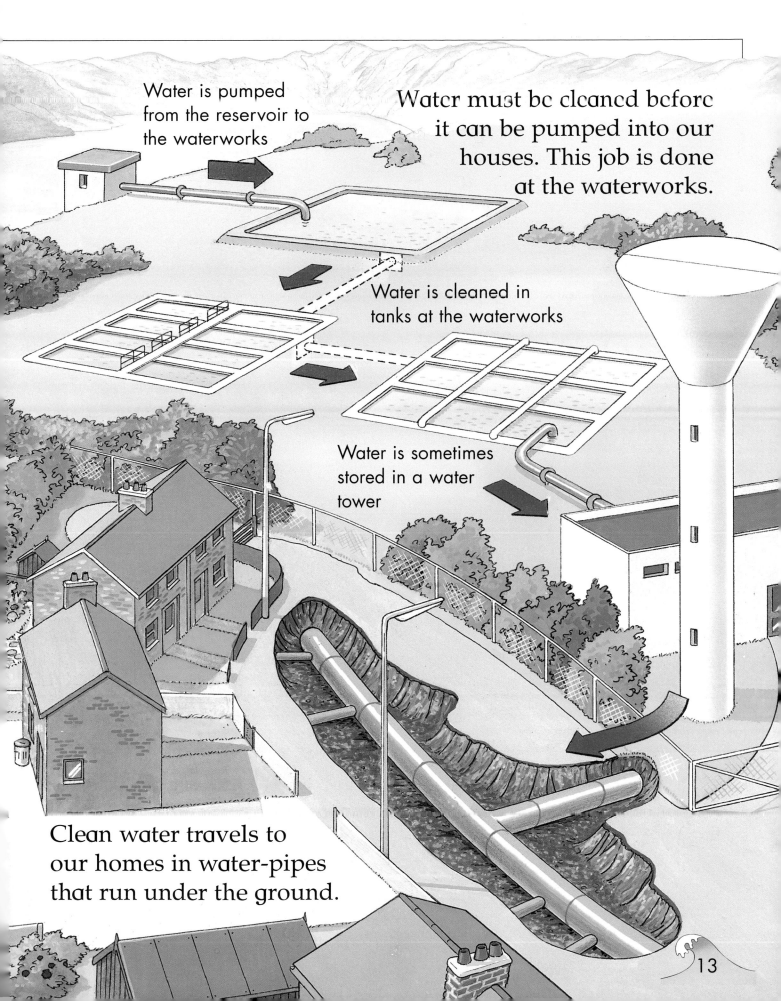

Water is pumped from the reservoir to the waterworks

Water must be cleaned before it can be pumped into our houses. This job is done at the waterworks.

Water is cleaned in tanks at the waterworks

Water is sometimes stored in a water tower

Clean water travels to our homes in water-pipes that run under the ground.

Washing

It is very important to keep our bodies clean and free from the germs that could make us ill.

It's easy for this elephant to keep itself clean, too.

Our clothes must be washed and dried when they are dirty.

Just think how dirty we would be without water.

Water can wash away most kinds of dirt except for greasy things like fat, wax or oil. We use soap to break up grease so that water can wash it away.

Detergents work like soap to help water to wash away grease.

WASHING UP

This will help you to understand why we need washing-up liquid to get the dishes really clean. Washing-up liquid contains detergent.

1 Fill a glass half full with cold water. Add some cold cooking oil. The oil will form a layer on top of the water. Even if you stir it up, the oil will always separate itself from the water.

2 Now add a few drops of washing-up liquid and notice what happens when you stir it in.

3 The detergent has broken up the oil so that the water can mix with it. This means that the water can now wash the oil away.

Down the Drain

Dirty water pours down the plug hole, down a pipe and out into the drain that runs under the ground outside your house.

Dirty water

Dirty water is cleaned at the sewage works

The water from your drain joins the **sewer** where it mixes with water from lots of other people's houses.

The sewer carries the dirty water to the sewage works. Here it is cleaned before being piped back into a river or the sea.

Clean water is piped into the river

Houses that are not connected to a sewer have their own **septic tank**. Water is purified in the tank before it soaks away into the ground.

Septic tank

Before drains were invented, people threw dirty water out of the house into the street. This made the streets smelly and unhealthy.

MAKE A FILTER

This activity will help you to understand **filtration**, which is one of the things that happens to the water at the sewage works.

1 Fill a jam jar with clean water and mix a spoonful of garden soil into it.

2 Now line a funnel with kitchen paper. The kitchen paper will act as a filter.

3 Place the funnel over a clean, empty jam jar. Pour the dirty water into the funnel.

4 The kitchen paper filters out the dirt. The water that drips into the jam jar will be clean.

Water Power

Water can be made to work for us. Water-wheels are used to drive many different kinds of machines.

Water from a river is made to fall on to the blades of a huge wheel.

The water falling on to the wheel makes it turn around.

The turning wheel is used to drive other machinery.

For thousands of years water-wheels were used in flour mills to drive the machines that crush corn and turn it into flour. In some parts of the world flour is still made using water power.

Today, water is often used to provide power for the machines that make electricity.

Fast-flowing water turns wheels called **turbines**. As the turbines turn around they drive electric **generators**.

Moving Force

Moving water is very powerful. When there is a flood, water can wash away houses, cars and even roads.

Generators make the electricity that we use in our homes and factories. Electricity made using water power is called hydroelectricity.

Floating

MAKE A CLAY BOAT

1 Fill a bowl with water and try to float a ball of modelling clay in it. Does it float?

2 Now push some of the clay out of the middle of your ball to make a hollow shape, like a boat. Does it float now?

3 Put a marble into your clay boat. How many marbles can it carry before it sinks? Too much cargo could make a ship sink.

Things float because water pushes up against them, supporting their weight. The force that pushes objects upwards is called upthrust.

It's incredible to think that huge, metal cargo ships weighing thousands of tonnes can float.

The upthrust of the water and the shape of the ship make it float.

Floating On Air

Filling things with air helps them to float. We use armbands filled with air to help us to swim. These lifeboatmen are rushing along in an air-filled dinghy.

The Salty Sea

Have you ever noticed how much easier it is to float in the sea than the swimming pool? This is because sea water is salty. Salt makes the upthrust of the water stronger. Seas and oceans are salty because all the rivers that feed into the sea wash salt out of the ground and carry it down to the sea.

The Dead Sea

The Dead Sea in Israel is extremely salty. People find it very easy to float in the salty water.

22

Salt disappears when it is mixed with water. This is called **dissolving**. When a substance dissolves in water the mixture is called a solution. Hot water dissolves things more quickly than cold.

MAKE A SOLUTION

1 Fill a glass with warm water. Add a teaspoonful of salt to the water and stir it up. Does the salt dissolve completely?

2 Repeat the experiment with sugar.

3 What happens when you mix mud with water? Does it disappear?

Unlike salt, mud does not dissolve completely in water.

Walking on Water

We can't walk on water but the pond skater can. If you look very carefully, you will see that its feet make tiny dents on the water's surface. It is as though the water were covered with a thin, stretchy skin. This effect is called surface tension. Surface tension is a force which holds water together.

If you look at a dripping tap you will see that the water drops are pear-shaped as they leave the tap. The force of surface tension pulls the drops into rounded shapes as they fall.

SURFACE TENSION

1 Fill a glass with water. Carefully add more water until you reach the top. You will find that the surface of the water is higher than the rim of the glass. Surface tension stops the water from overflowing.

2 Surface tension is strong enough to support a paper clip. Take a small piece of paper towel and float it in a glass of water. Place the paper clip gently on the paper. Soon the paper will sink, leaving the clip floating on the water.

This huge soap bubble is made from soapy water pulled together by surface tension.

Even bubbles of this size will become rounded when they are let go.

Under Pressure

When you dive under water, it pushes against you from all directions. The push is called water pressure. The deeper you dive, the greater the pressure of the water is.

Humans cannot dive deeper than 120 metres without wearing special suits. Deep sea divers wear thick suits which stop their bodies being crushed by the pressure of the water.

Deep-sea Angler Fish

Fish that live at the bottom of the ocean are specially adapted to withstand the pressure of the water. The pressure inside their bodies is equal to the water pressure outside. If they were brought to the surface, this pressure would make their bodies explode.

Submarines can go even deeper under the water. They have thick, strong metal hulls which cannot be crushed by the pressure of the water.

The bathyscaphe is built to withstand enormous water pressure. In 1960 the Swiss explorer Jaques Piccard broke all records with the crew of the US bathyscaphe *Trieste* when they dived 11km below the surface of the Pacific.

Staying Dry

Some materials soak up water. We call these permeable materials. Other materials won't let water through them at all. These are called waterproof materials.

Fishermen and sailors need waterproof clothes to keep them warm and dry. Some clothes are made waterproof by coating them with wax. The wax stops the water from soaking into the material.

TESTING WATERPROOF MATERIALS

1 Put a small plastic funnel into a jar.

2 Line the funnel with a plastic bag, covering the hole at the bottom completely.

3 Pour the water slowly into the funnel until it is full. Does any of the water escape?

4 Now line the funnel with paper. What happens to the water?

5 Try lining the funnel with fabric, covering the hole again.

Plastic is waterproof. That is why the water cannot soak through it. Paper and most fabrics are permeable. This means that they allow water to soak through them.

Many birds and animals have their own waterproof coats. A duck's feathers are coated in oil which makes them waterproof.

Living in Water

Millions of different creatures live under water in ponds, rivers, oceans and even puddles. Some of them are so small that we can only see them through a microscope.

All living things need oxygen. Oxygen can dissolve in water. Fish collect the oxygen they need using their **gills**.

A fish's gills are just behind its head. The fish breathes by taking water into its mouth and washing it over its gills. The gills collect oxygen from the water.

Heavy Weight

Water can support the weight of very large creatures. The blue whale is the largest creature that has ever lived. Imagine how big its legs would need to be if it lived on dry land!

Glossary

Bore hole: A very deep, narrow hole made in the earth to reach water under the ground

Condensation: The change of a gas or a vapour in to a liquid

Dam: A barrier built across a river to stop flooding, create a reservoir or make hydroelectricity

Droplets: Tiny drops of water

Evaporation: The change of liquid into a gas or vapour

Filtration: The removal of solid materials from a liquid

Fuels: Materials that can be burnt to produce heat or power

Generator: A machine for turning water power into electricity

Gills: A fish's gills are behind its head. They are covered with a special skin which takes in oxygen from the water

Pollute: To make dirty or poison with chemicals, sewage or other kinds of waste

Reservoir: An artificial lake for storing water

Septic tank: A tank in which sewage is broken down and cleaned by bacteria

Sewer: A large, underground pipe used to carry sewage away from houses

Turbine: A machine with many blades that turn to make electricity

Water vapour: Tiny, invisible drops of water in the air

Index

Bathyscaphe 27
Boiling 7, 8
Bore hole 12

Condensation 7, 9

Dams 12
Dead Sea 22
Deep-sea angler fish 27
Detergent 15
Dissolving 22-23
Duck 29
Drains 16, 17

Electricity 19
Evaporation 8-9, 11

Filters 17
Fish 30
Floating 20-22
Floods 19

Generators 19
Geysers 5

Ice 6, 7, 10

Lakes 8

Oceans 4, 9, 11, 26-27

Rain 10
Reservoirs 12
Rivers 8, 10, 11

Septic tank 17
Sewer 16
Ships 20-21
Snow 10, 12
Soap 15
Solution 23
Submarines 27
Surface tension 24-25
Steam 7

Turbines 19

Upthrust 20

Washing 14-15
Water cycle 10-11
Water pressure 26-27
Waterproof 28-29
Water vapour 7, 8-9, 10
Water-wheels 18
Waterworks 13
Well 12
Whales 31